D1404201

Fact Finders®

MILITARY HEROES

# SEAL TEAM

## BATTLING TERRORISM WORLDWIDE

# SIX

BY JOHN MICKLOS, JR.

CONSULTANT:
RAYMOND L. PUFFER, PHD
HISTORIAN, RETIRED
EDWARDS AIR FORCE BASE HISTORY OFFICE

CAPSTONE PRESS
a capstone imprint

**Fact Finders Books are published by Capstone Press,**
**1710 Roe Crest Drive, North Mankato, Minnesota 56003**
**www.mycapstone.com**

**Library of Congress Cataloging-in-Publication Data**
Names: Micklos, John, author.
Title: SEAL Team Six : battling terrorism worldwide / by John Micklos, Jr.
Description: North Mankato, Minnesota : Capstone Press, [2017] | Series: Fact
   finders. Military heroes | Includes bibliographical references and index.
   | Audience: Grades 4-6.
Identifiers: LCCN 2016027449 |
ISBN 9781515733478 (library binding) |
ISBN 9781515733492 (eBook PDF)
Subjects: LCSH: : LCSH: United States. Navy. SEALs—Juvenile literature. | United States. Navy—Commando troops—Biography—Juvenile literature. | United States. Naval Special Warfare Development Group—Juvenile literature.
Classification: LCC VG87 .M58 2017 | DDC 359.9/84—dc23
LC record available at https://lccn.loc.gov/2016027449

**Editorial Credits**
Editor: Brenda Haugen
Designers: Kayla Dohmen and Kristi Carlson
Media Researcher: Ruth Smith
Production Specialist: Tori Abraham

**Photo Credits**
Alamy: Oleg Zabielin, cover; Getty Images: Agence France Presse, 10, BAY ISMOYO/AFP, 28, Bettmann, 9, HOCINE ZAOURAR/AFP, 22, Steven D Starr, 19, The Washington Post, 12-13; Navy SEAL Museum: 7; Newscom: AARHUS/SIPA, 18, Department of Defense – CNP, 24, Jon Mitchell/Photoshot, 21, PSG, 17, SIPA USA/SIPA, 25, US Navy/AFLO, 14; Shutterstock: Andy Dean Photography, 23, Carolina K. Smith MD, 27, MilanTomazin, 5

**Primary source bibliography**
Page 6—O'Donnell, Patrick K. *The Untold Story of the Forging of America's Most Elite Unit.* Philadelphia: Da Capo Press, 2014.
Page 13—Hollenbeck, Cliff, and Dick Couch. *To Be a U.S. Navy SEAL.* St. Paul, Minn.: MBI Publishing, 2003.
Page 14—Pfarrer, Chuck. *SEAL Target Geronimo: The Inside Story of the Mission to Kill Osama bin Laden.* New York: St. Martin's Press, 2011.
Page 15—Navy Seals.com. http://navyseals.com/nsw/seal-code-warrior-creed/. Retrieved July 26, 2016.
Page 16—Mann, Don. with Ralph Pezzullo. *Inside SEAL Team Six: My Life and Missions with America's Elite Warriors.* New York: Little, Brown, 2011.
Page 23—Wasdin, Howard E., and Stephen Templin. *SEAL Team Six: Memoirs of an Elite Navy SEAL Sniper.* New York: St. Martin's Press, 2011.
Page 27—Schmidle, Nicholas. "Getting bin Laden." *The New Yorker.* August 8, 2011. Retrieved July 26, 2016. www.newyorker.com/magazine/2011/08/08/getting-bin-laden
Page 29—"In Somalia, Surviving Against 'Impossible Odds.'" *Morning Edition.* May 14, 2013. Retrieved July 26, 2016. www.npr.org/2013/05/14/183624076/in-somalia-surviving-a-kidnapping-against-impossible-odds

Printed and bound in China.
009943S17

# TABLE OF CONTENTS

# CHAPTER 1

# Origins of the SEALs

Conducting top secret missions. Slipping behind enemy lines. Rescuing heads of state and kidnap victims. Killing terrorist leaders. Sounds like a James Bond movie, right? Think again. Those are routine days for the U.S. Navy's highly trained SEAL Team Six special operations force.

SEAL Team Six members have been involved in some of the world's most spectacular missions in recent decades. They include the killing of al-Qaida leader Osama bin Laden in 2011 and the rescue of Captain Richard Phillips of the *Maersk Alabama* from Somali pirates in 2009.

The operations and the publicity that followed have brought increased attention to a unit that prides itself on working in secrecy. But what exactly is SEAL Team Six, and how did it begin?

The concept for the SEALs began during World War II as the United States fought against Germany and Japan. Newly developed underwater breathing equipment allowed specially trained U.S. Navy divers to swim underwater without leaving behind a trail of bubbles. Soon the men were conducting secret missions against both the Germans and the Japanese.

## Did You Know?

Navy divers during World War II were often called frogmen because they operated both in the water and on land.

A frogman in complete diving gear held his weapon at the ready.

Highly trained naval combat **demolition** units (NCDUs) led the way for the famed D-Day invasion on June 6, 1944. The NCDUs marked and disabled German explosives. This helped U.S. soldiers and their allies overrun the German defenses at Normandy, France. It marked a key turning point in helping the Allies win the war.

Other Navy teams carried out missions in the Pacific Ocean region, where the Allies were battling the Japanese. Team members faced extreme danger.

*"You are not alive, unless you are living on the edge."*

—*World War II Navy team member Walter Mess*

**demolition**—the act of destroying something

## THE FIRST SEAL

A U.S. Navy dentist named Jack Taylor is considered the nation's first SEAL. During World War II, he was trained in using the Navy's new underwater breathing equipment. He used that training and his skill in guiding small boats to conduct daring wartime missions. He delivered ammunition and supplies to help the Allies free Greece from German control. The Germans later captured and tortured Taylor. According to the Navy SEAL Museum, Taylor's "exploits and personal daring serve as a role model for present day SEALs."

The U.S. Navy used rubber boats as landing crafts during World War II.

# CHAPTER 2

# SEAL TEAM SIX

The World War II U.S. Navy frogmen were the **forerunners** to the SEALs. The term SEAL, however, did not appear until 1961. It was used to describe a new type of unit that would specialize in **amphibious** landings and especially dangerous and difficult missions. The name SEAL comes from the fact that the unit would include elements of sea, air, and land.

The first SEALs began operations in 1962 during the Vietnam War. At first they worked to clear North Vietnamese **guerrilla** forces—called Viet Cong—from around Saigon, the capital of South Vietnam. Later, the SEALs extended their raids farther out into the countryside. Moving quietly, small teams of SEALs ambushed Viet Cong fighters. The Viet Cong called them "the men with green faces" because of their **camouflage**. The SEALs were among the most highly decorated small units in the conflict.

**forerunner**—something or someone that comes before and prepares the way
**amphibious**—describes a type of vehicle or craft that can travel over land and also over or in water
**guerrilla**—a member of a small group of fighters or soldiers
**camouflage**—patterns and colors designed to make military personnel, uniforms, gear, and weapons blend in with a natural setting

American troops crouched down low after being dropped by helicopter into an area where enemy weapons were being fired.

The more specialized, highly secretive SEAL Team Six was formed in 1980. Iranian students had seized the U.S. Embassy in Tehran in November 1979. They held 52 American hostages for more than a year. President Jimmy Carter authorized a rescue mission called Operation Eagle Claw in April 1980. The mission was cut short because of the failure of three of the eight helicopters. Eight servicemen died when one of the helicopters crashed into a transport aircraft. Six months later the U.S. Navy created SEAL Team Six to combat global terrorism and handle specialized missions.

SEAL Team Six was dissolved in 1987. It was replaced by the Naval Special Warfare Development Group (DEVGRU). Many people still refer to the group as SEAL Team Six, though.

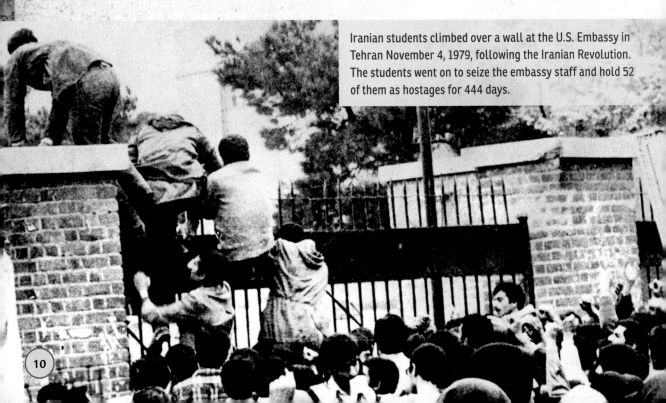

Iranian students climbed over a wall at the U.S. Embassy in Tehran November 4, 1979, following the Iranian Revolution. The students went on to seize the embassy staff and hold 52 of them as hostages for 444 days.

# SEAL TIMELINE

Key dates and missions in SEAL/SEAL Team Six history:

## 1944
Naval combat demolition units (NCDUs) disable German explosives to help the Allied landing at Normandy succeed; they also conduct many other missions during World War II

## 1961
The term SEAL first appears

## 1962
The first SEAL units begin operation in Vietnam

## 1980
After an attempt to free U.S. hostages in Iran fails, SEAL Team Six is formed to conduct especially dangerous and difficult special missions

## 1983
SEAL Team Six conducts a mission to rescue the governor general of Grenada after **resistance** fighters try to take over the government of the Caribbean country

## 1987
SEAL Team Six is dissolved; it is replaced by the Naval Special Warfare Development Group (DEVGRU), but the name SEAL Team Six is still frequently used

## 1989
SEAL Team Six members play a key role in Operation Just Cause to capture General Manuel Noriega, the military dictator of Panama

## 1993
SEAL Team Six is involved in the Battle of Mogadishu in Somalia

## 2001
Throughout the war in Afghanistan, SEAL Team Six members conduct many operations against the Taliban and al-Qaida

## 2003
SEAL Team Six members conduct missions during the Iraq War that topples dictator Saddam Hussein

## 2009
SEAL Team Six members rescue Captain Richard Phillips from Somali pirates

## 2011
SEAL Team Six members kill al-Qaida leader Osama bin Laden at his hideout in Pakistan

## 2011
Fifteen SEAL Team Six members are among the 38 casualties when the Taliban shoot down a U.S. helicopter in Afghanistan

## 2012
SEAL Team Six members rescue American aid worker Jessica Buchanan from pirates in Somalia

## 2014
Two separate SEAL Team Six rescue missions in Yemen succeed in rescuing several hostages, but the kidnappers kill American hostage Luke Somers

## 2016
Edward C. Byers Jr. is believed to be the first member of SEAL Team Six to win the Medal of Honor, the highest award in the United States for valor in combat; he earned the honor for his part in a hostage-rescue mission in Afghanistan in 2012

---

**resistance**—a fighting force opposed to the government

# CHAPTER 3

# ELITE OF THE ELITE

Many people apply to become Navy SEALs. Few make it through the tough training process. In fact, fewer than 250 graduate from the six-month SEAL basic training each year. How **elite** are the SEALs? More than 300,000 men and women serve in the U.S. Navy. Only about 2,500 can call themselves SEALs. That's fewer than one in 100.

SEAL training classes take place in California throughout the year. For years, only male members of the U.S. Navy ages 18 through 28 could apply (17 with parental permission). Beginning in 2016 women could apply as well. To qualify for SEAL training, applicants must pass a tough fitness test. It involves doing at least 50 pushups and 50 sit-ups within two-minute time periods.

**elite**—a group of people who have special advantages or talents

Candidates must be able to do at least 10 pull-ups. They have to swim 500 yards (457 meters) within 12 ½ minutes. And they have to run 1 ½ miles (2.4 kilometers) in 10 ½ minutes or less. The test weeds out many candidates before the actual training even begins.

The candidates who qualify face an intensive seven-week training course. They practice running, swimming, and crawling through all sorts of conditions. They push their bodies to their limits—and beyond. Training begins with Basic Underwater Demolition/SEAL

(BUDS) training. "SEAL training ... is designed to create warriors," wrote former SEAL Dick Couch. Throughout training, instructors stress the importance of teamwork. On dangerous missions, working together can mean the difference between life and death.

> *"(The training) is a sorting process that finds young men who would rather die than quit."*
>
> —*former SEAL Dick Couch*

Navy SEALs performed a demonstration at Howard University. A part of the demonstration was showing those involved how difficult SEAL training is.

Week 4 is called Hell Week. Applicants have to perform all their duties on a total of less than five hours of sleep over five days.

*"The survivors look like shipwreck victims. But all of them have one thing in common——they did not, and would not, quit."*

—former SEAL Team Six member Chuck Pfarrer talking about Hell Week

Applicants took part in physical training at Naval Amphibious Base Coronado in California.

# More Training

Those who make it through the seven-week course face even more training. They learn specialized skills such as scuba diving. To pass this phase of training, they must swim and float—with their hands and feet tied together. SEAL trainees then practice land warfare. They train with a variety of weapons. They practice hand-to-hand combat.

After six months of basic training comes—still more training. At this point, trainees begin six months of SEAL Qualification Training (SQT). They work to perfect the skills they have learned. They also jump out of airplanes to practice using parachutes. Fewer than one in three candidates makes it through all phases of training. Those who do make it earn the **trident** pin and can call themselves SEALs. Each day they strive to live up to the SEAL code, which ends with the words: "Brave men have fought and died building the proud tradition and feared reputation that I am bound to uphold. In the worst of conditions, the **legacy** of my teammates steadies my resolve and silently guides my every deed. I will not fail."

## Did You Know?

The trident symbol on the SEAL pin links to Greek mythology. Poseidon, the Greek god of the sea, used a trident.

**trident**—a long spear with three sharp points at its end
**legacy**—qualities or actions that one is remembered for; something that is passed on to future generations

# THE BEST OF THE BEST

|||||||||||||||||||||||||||||||||||||||||||||||||||||||||||||||||||||||||||||||

From the elite group of SEALs comes the even more elite SEAL Team Six. DEVGRU recruits only from among those who have already served as SEALs for several years. Candidates undergo extreme training over a period of more than six months. They learn to parachute accurately from 30,000 feet (9 km), strapped to an oxygen tank. Constant practice further sharpens their shooting skills. Only about half of the recruits qualify to serve. No one knows exactly how many members the team has.

*"You can't anticipate the challenges that are going to be thrown your way. All you can do is prepare yourself to the best of your abilities."*

—Dan Mann, who served as an active duty SEAL for 25 years

U.S. Navy personnel practiced parachuting in the Pacific Ocean.

# CHAPTER 4

# MAJOR MISSIONS

Over the years SEAL Team Six has been involved in a number of successful, high-profile missions across the world. SEAL Team Six worked with just a few hours' notice to rescue Governor General Paul Scoon of Grenada in October 1983. He had been captured by people who wanted to take over the government of the tiny Caribbean island.

The United States invaded Panama in December 1989. The goal of Operation Just Cause was to capture General Manuel Noriega, the country's military dictator. Noriega had ruled harshly. He also trafficked drugs. SEALs played a key role in his capture. They disabled the boat and airplane he might have used to escape. Four SEALs died in the airfield raid. Noriega later served many years in prison for his criminal activities.

General Manuel Noriega

American soldiers patrolled the streets of Panama after the U.S. invasion of the country in 1989.

# MORE IMPORTANT MISSIONS

After the September 11 terror attacks in 2001, SEALs conducted operations in Afghanistan against the Taliban. These Muslim extremists had provided shelter for Osama bin Laden to plan his terror attacks.

SEAL Team Six members helped support the U.S. military campaign to install a democracy in Afghanistan. SEALs also played a role in helping to topple dictator Saddam Hussein during the Iraq invasion in 2003.

In recent years SEALs have played key roles in rescue operations in Somalia, Afghanistan, and Yemen. Often, they rescue aid workers or other hostages who had been captured by terrorists. The most famous rescue came in 2009. Somali pirates had captured the *Maersk Alabama* and were holding Captain Richard Phillips hostage. One pirate surrendered. SEAL **marksmen** killed the other three with single shots.

**marksman**—a person skilled at aiming and shooting guns

The lifeboat (left) where Captain Richard Phillips was held hostage was processed for evidence after his rescue.

# MOVIE MANIA

Top secret missions. Rapid-fire action. SEAL Team Six operations provide great material for movies. In recent years their missions have sparked several popular movies. *Zero Dark Thirty* (2012) tells the behind-the-scenes story of the mission to kill Osama bin Laden. It focuses mostly on the detailed planning that led to the mission, but there's action too. *Captain Phillips* (2013) details the mission to rescue the captain and crew of the *Maersk Alabama* from Somali pirates. The movie focuses on the captain's efforts to keep his crew alive, but it also spotlights the brave work of the SEALs.

# DANGEROUS WORK

Most SEAL Team Six missions are both complex and dangerous. The SEALs must plan for all possibilities. Despite their careful preparation, things sometimes go wrong. For instance, in 1993, the United States tried to help bring order to war-torn Somalia. At the Battle of Mogadishu in Somalia in 1993, two Black Hawk helicopters were shot down. Several SEALs died in the fighting.

American United Nations soldiers patrolled Mogadishu, Somalia, in October 1993.

An attempt in 2010 to rescue kidnapped Scottish aid worker Linda Norgrove in Pakistan failed when a grenade landed near her and killed her. Fifteen members of DEVGRU's Gold Squadron were among 38 soldiers who died in 2011 when the Taliban shot down a Chinook helicopter in Afghanistan.

Most people think of SEAL Team Six as deadly. But they kill only when necessary. "If you can do an op without any loss of life, it's a great op," said former SEAL sniper Howard E. Wasdin. Seriously wounded at the Battle of Mogadishu, Wasdin received the Purple Heart, a U.S. military decoration given to those wounded or killed in action.

Despite the extreme danger, most SEAL Team Six missions end successfully. The team's most famous success came on May 2, 2011, in Pakistan with the killing of al-Qaida leader Osama bin Laden.

Purple Heart war medal

# CHAPTER 5

# GETTING BIN LADEN

For a decade Osama bin Laden had lived as the world's most wanted man. The United States offered a reward of $25 million for information leading to the capture of the al-Qaida leader who masterminded the September 11 terrorist attacks. By spring 2010, the United States had information suggesting that bin Laden was living in a compound in Abbottabad, Pakistan. The government worked to confirm that lead.

Osama bin Laden was killed in his compound in Pakistan.

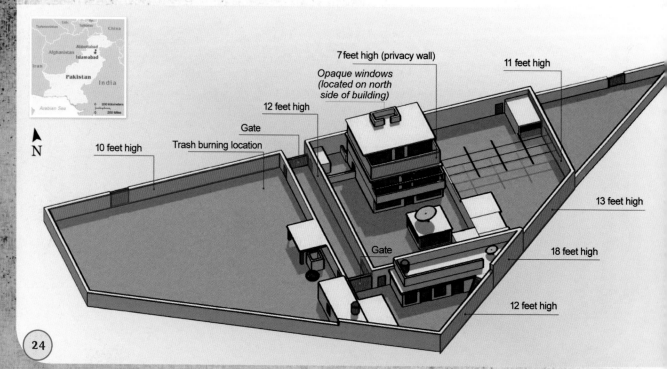

7 feet high (privacy wall)

Opaque windows
(located on north
side of building)

11 feet high

12 feet high

Gate

10 feet high

Trash burning location

13 feet high

Gate

18 feet high

12 feet high

N

President Barack Obama (second from left) monitored the mission to get Osama bin Laden.

Meanwhile, DEVGRU team members began training for a top-secret mission. They practiced assaulting a life-sized three-dimensional model of the one-acre (0.4 hectare) compound they would be raiding. At first they did not know what the compound was. But they suspected it might be a model of bin Laden's hideout.

The team transferred to Jalalabad, Afghanistan, on April 26, 2011. Late on Sunday night, May 1, two DEVGRU assault teams of 24 members flew undetected about 90 miles (145 km) to bin Laden's compound. Two Black Hawk helicopters carrying one assault team arrived at bin Laden's compound around 1:00 a.m. The other three helicopters and the second group of 24 SEALs remained ready a short distance away. Back in the United States, President Barack Obama and other top officials waited anxiously for news in the White House.

# THE BEST IN THE WORLD

The carefully planned attack faced challenges. One helicopter lost its lift and made a hard landing in the compound. The other landed outside. Using explosives, the team inside the compound blew its way into the main house. Moving room by room, team members worked their way to the third floor. They believed bin Laden would be there.

Bin Laden saw them coming and ducked into a nearby room. SEAL Team Six members quickly followed. They shot him when they believed he might be reaching for a gun. They photographed the body and took DNA samples for testing. By satellite radio they reported that bin Laden had been killed. The listeners in the White House celebrated.

SEAL Team Six grabbed computers, thumb drives, and disks and prepared to leave. The entire raid had lasted only 40 minutes. A reserve helicopter came to get them. They blew up the downed Black Hawk helicopter so enemies couldn't make use of it. There were no American casualties.

Newspapers all across the United States reported on the death of Osama bin Laden.

Within a few hours, news of bin Laden's death made headlines around the world. Within a few days, word leaked that SEAL Team Six members had conducted the mission. Back in the United States, President Obama met with members of the SEAL team. "I had fifty-fifty confidence that bin Laden was there, but I had one hundred percent confidence in you guys," Obama said. "You are, literally, the finest small-fighting force that has ever existed in the world."

# CHAPTER 6

# CONTINUING OPERATIONS

Since the bin Laden mission, SEAL Team Six has struggled to keep its secrecy. Books and movies have detailed their work. Some books have been written by current or former SEAL Team Six members. For instance, the bestselling book *No Easy Day: The Firsthand Account of the Mission that Killed Osama bin Laden* by Mark Owen and Kevin Maurer provided an insider's account of the bin Laden raid.

Through it all SEAL Team Six has continued to conduct missions. In 2012 SEAL Team Six members rescued aid workers Jessica Buchanan and Poul Thisted from pirates in Somalia. Later that year, team members rescued American Dr. Dilip Joseph from the Taliban in Afghanistan. During the mission, they killed seven Taliban and captured two others. One SEAL Team Six member, Nicolas Checque, died during the rescue.

SEALs train anti-terror troops from other countries in an effort to stop terrorism around the world.

In late 2014, SEAL Team Six launched two separate missions to rescue hostages held by al-Qaida in Yemen. During the first mission, they freed eight hostages. But American hostage Luke Somers and the other remaining hostage, Pierre Korkie of South Africa, were shot by their captors during the second rescue attempt. Both died.

SEAL Team Six has had a colorful history. Its members have been involved in some of the world's most daring and successful special operations missions. What about the future? As the worldwide battle against terrorism continues to heat up, it seems certain that many more missions lie ahead.

## VIEW FROM A HOSTAGE

Somali pirates kidnapped two aid workers—Jessica Buchanan of the United States and Poul Thisted of Denmark—in October 2011. The pirates held the two hostages for more than three months. They sought millions of dollars in ransom money. Buchanan suffered from a kidney ailment. Lacking proper medication, she grew gravely ill. SEAL Team Six launched a lightning strike on January 24, 2012. Within minutes all nine pirates lay dead. The SEALs quickly moved the hostages to safety. Buchanan later recalled, "One of them just scoops me up, I mean, like a movie, and just, you know, runs across the desert with me to a safe place." One of them even went back to the camp and retrieved a ring she had left behind.

# GLOSSARY

**amphibious** (am-FI-bee-uhs)—describes a type of vehicle or craft that can travel over land and also over or in water

**camouflage** (KA-muh-flahzh)—patterns and colors designed to make military personnel, uniforms, gear, and weapons blend in with a natural setting

**demolition** (de-muh-LI-shuhn)—the act of destroying something

**elite** (i-LEET)—a group of people who have special advantages or talents

**forerunner** (FOHR-ruhn-ur)—something or someone that comes before and prepares the way

**guerrilla** (guh-RIL-ah)—a member of a small group of fighters or soldiers

**legacy** (LAY-guh-see)—qualities or actions that one is remembered for; something that is passed on to future generations

**marksman** (MARKS-muhn)—a person skilled at aiming and shooting guns

**resistance** (ri-ZISS-tuhnss)—a fighting force opposed to the government

**trident** (TRIy-dent)—a long spear with three sharp points at its end

# READ MORE

**George, Enzo.** *The Afghanistan and Iraq Wars: War Against Extremism.* Voices of War. New York: Cavendish Square Publishing, 2015.

**Newman, Patricia.** *Navy SEALs: Elite Operations.* Military Special Ops. Minneapolis: Lerner Publications, 2014.

**Person, Stephen.** *Navy SEAL Team Six in Action.* Special Ops II. New York: Bearport Publishing, 2014.

# INTERNET SITES

FactHound offers a safe, fun way to find Internet sites related to this book. All of the sites on FactHound have been researched by our staff.

Here's all you do:
Visit **www.facthound.com**
Type in this code: 9781515733478

Check out projects, games and lots more at
**www.capstonekids.com**

# CRITICAL THINKING USING THE COMMON CORE

1. What makes membership on SEAL Team Six so elite? (Key Ideas and Details)

2. Why is the role of SEAL Team Six likely to remain so important in the years to come? (Integration of Knowledge of Ideas)

3. How are hostage rescue missions similar to and different from missions such as the one targeting Osama bin Laden? (Craft and Structure)

# INDEX